10/13

FOSSIL RIDGE PUBLIC LIBRARY DISTRICT

W9-BTQ-775

An enemy is a person whose story we have not heard.

—Gene Knudsen Hoffman, American peace activist and author (1919–2010)

For Jack, with a lot of love and the earnest hope that the world can work things out.

Text © 2013 Niki Walker

All rights reserved. No part of this publication may be reproduced, stored in a retrieval system, or transmitted in any form or by any means, without the prior written permission of Owlkids Books Inc., or in the case of photocopying or other reprographic copying, a license from the Canadian Copyright Licensing Agency (Access Copyright). For an Access Copyright license, visit www.accesscopyright.ca or call toll-free to 1-800-893-5777.

Owlkids Books acknowledges the financial support of the Canada Council for the Arts, the Ontario Arts Council, the Government of Canada through the Canada Book Fund (CBF) and the Government of Ontario through the Ontario Media Development Corporation's Book Initiative for our publishing activities.

Published in Canada by
Owlkids Books Inc.
10 Lower Spadina Avenue
Toronto, ON M5V 2Z2

Published in the United States by
Owlkids Books Inc.
1700 Fourth Street
Berkeley, CA 94710

Library and Archives Canada Cataloguing in Publication

Walker, Niki, 1972-
    Why do we fight? : conflict, war, and peace / Niki Walker.

Includes bibliographical references and index.
ISBN 978-1-926973-86-9

    1. Conflict management--Juvenile literature.
2. Fighting (Psychology)--Juvenile literature 3. War--Juvenile literature. 4. Peace--Juvenile literature.
I. Title.

HM1126.W36 2013   j303.6'9   C2012-908518-9

Library of Congress Control Number: 2013930981

Design: Barb Kelly

Manufactured in North Point, Hong Kong, in March 2013, by Sheck Wah Tong Printing Press Ltd.
Job #66618

A   B   C   D   E   F

 Publisher of Chirp, chickaDEE and OWL
www.owlkidsbooks.com

FOSSIL RIDGE PUBLIC LIBRARY DISTRICT
BRAIDWOOD, IL 60408

WHY Do We FIGHT?

Conflict, War, and Peace

By Niki Walker

CONTENTS

introduction

No matter how thin you slice it, there will always be two sides

—Baruch Spinoza, Jewish-Dutch philosopher (1632–77)

What Is CONFLICT?

Battles, protests, standoffs, strikes.

You hear about them all the time. On the surface, a battle and a protest don't seem to have much in common, right?

A battle involves guns and bombs, while a protest has signs and picket lines. But they're really just two ways of handling a dispute. One uses violence, and the other doesn't (or not in most cases, anyway). Both start as a disagreement between two groups of people.

BOTH ARE CONFLICTS.

So have you been part of any conflicts this week?

Before you say no, stop and think about it.

Did you agree with everything everyone around you said?

Did you feel like doing everything people asked you to?

> **Con·flict:**
> An intense disagreement that can lead either to violence or to a peaceful solution, depending on how it's handled.

Unless you're the only person—ever—who's okay with everything going on around you, chances are pretty good you've been in a disagreement before. Maybe you had a fight with your sibling over what to watch on TV. Or maybe a kid in math class wanted to cheat off your test but you didn't want her to.

Since it's impossible for people to agree on everything all the time, conflicts naturally pop up anywhere people get thrown together—at school, at work, at home, in big cities and small towns and whole countries. Conflicts are part of life.

No one really likes conflict, but disagreements don't always have to be violent. Or even unpleasant. They can be a chance to make changes happen—if the people involved are willing to listen and work things out. The way a conflict gets resolved, or settled, depends on how the people involved handle it. Sometimes conflicts get resolved by talking them out before they blow up into major fights. Sometimes they get settled by fighting. That's true of conflicts between people on the street. It's also true of conflicts between countries on the world stage, too. We call those conflicts global conflicts.

When we talk about global conflicts, we're talking about major disagreements that get the world's attention. These break out among groups of people inside a country's borders or between countries. They are disputes that involve many thousands or even millions of people. And yes, global conflicts often get violent. Sometimes they turn into full-blown wars. They're a lot trickier to understand than the conflicts that come up in everyday life—and even trickier to settle.

So how can we even start to understand global conflicts and how they get resolved? By breaking them down into their basic parts. Look at the facing page to see what those parts are and learn how they fit together.

Meet a
GLOBAL
Conflict

Glo·bal con·flict: An often violent disagreement between countries or groups within countries that gets the world's attention and sometimes, involvement.

Although most conflicts around the world—from all-out wars to arguments over trading—are unique, they actually all have the same basic parts.

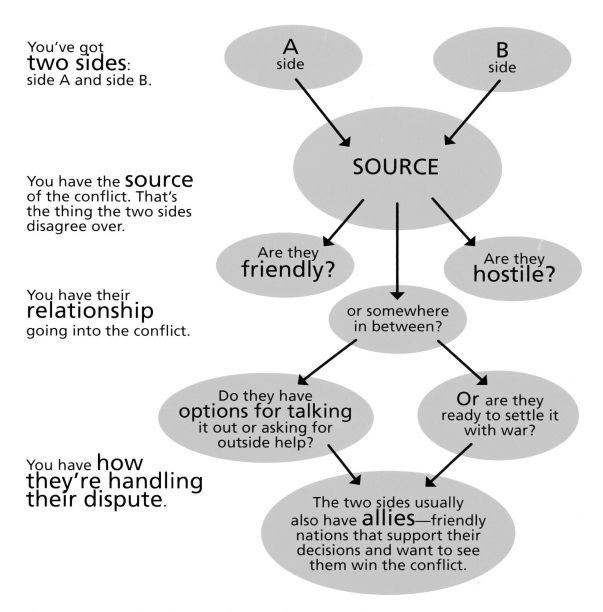

You've got **two sides**: side A and side B.

You have the **source** of the conflict. That's the thing the two sides disagree over.

You have their **relationship** going into the conflict.

You have **how they're handling their dispute**.

A side

B side

SOURCE

Are they **friendly?**

Are they **hostile?**

or somewhere in between?

Do they have **options for talking** it out or asking for outside help?

Or are they ready to settle it with war?

The two sides usually also have **allies**—friendly nations that support their decisions and want to see them win the conflict.

If you want to begin to understand any conflict, you need to start with the source—that is, what the countries or groups are fighting over. That's the root of the conflict, and it's not always easy to determine. Often, the source of a conflict isn't quite what you think it is, and there can be more than one source, too.

But even though there are many conflicts in the world—over different issues, between different countries, and involving different groups of people—when you get right down to it, they all start for a lot of the same reasons.

chapter 1

Honest disagreement is often a good sign of progress.

—Mahatma Gandhi, leader of Indian independence movement (1869–1948)

WHY DO CONFLICTS Come Up?

Every fight is about something, right? So what are global conflicts about?

At their core—whether they involve two people or two million—all conflicts are about people getting in the way of something someone else wants or needs.

Wants are things that don't really do anything to keep you alive, but they sure make life more enjoyable and comfortable. Things like cool sneakers or a video game.

Needs are part of the basic everyday business of staying alive. They include things like food and water and shelter.

Many wants and needs are physical—you can see them and touch them. But there are needs and wants you can't actually see that are just as important. They include things like freedom, security, and equality. You may not think about those things much if you're lucky enough to live in a country where they're protected.

Now imagine living in a place where you're not allowed to go to school because of your background. Or where you're always afraid of being attacked because of your race or religion. Or where you barely have enough food to survive. For many people, these are everyday sources of conflict.

Most global conflicts aren't about just one thing. When you start to look closely, you're likely to find there is a lot at stake, including some or all of the following:

LAND! POWER! EQUALITY!
RESOURCES! SECURITY!

In fact, these things are so closely tied to one another that it's often impossible to separate them. Yes, every fight is about something. But rarely is a fight about one thing.

E·qual·i·ty: The state of things when people have the same rights and the same opportunities, no matter what their background, religion, or gender is.

Se·cu·ri·ty: The feeling that you have everything you need and that you're safe.

A Place to Plant Your **FEET,** Your **FLAG,** And Your **FOOD**

Think for a second about what's under your feet. I don't mean the floor or the dust bunnies or the basement, but what's under all of those things: land.

Chances are hundreds or even thousands of years ago, someone fought over the very land you're on right now. That's because people have battled over land throughout history—and even before there was history.

Land = Wealth

For thousands of years, people conquered each other to get what they wanted. Usually what they wanted was more wealth, and the way to get that was by getting more land—and all the goodies that went with it.

Winner takes all

Con·quer:
To take over a land and its people using force.

Conquerors invaded a place, fought its people until they gave up, and then claimed the territory for themselves. The winners then made rules for the people living there, and they often set up a colony (meaning they controlled the area).

For the conquerors, plundering (or taking whatever they wanted) was part of the deal. At the end of battles and wars, the winners packed up whatever loot there was to be had—from grain and livestock to gold and artwork—and carted it home over land or sea.

The earliest war anyone ever wrote about was fought in 2700 BCE—not long after writing was invented. The war was between Sumer (in present-day Iraq) and Elam (in modern-day Iran). Judging by the descriptions written at the time, it seems like land and resources were major causes.

Land conflicts today

Most world leaders today agree that it's not acceptable to go around conquering people and claiming land to get what they want. But that doesn't mean people aren't still fighting over land. Most land conflicts today aren't between separate countries—they're between groups of people living within a country.

Why is land so important, anyway?

There are a few reasons why so many conflicts center around land disputes.

- First of all, you can't have much of a country (or kingdom, or empire) without some land to call your own. You need somewhere to plant your flag and build your castle, right?

- Then there are all the valuable things that go along with having land, like the resources found on it and under it—forests, farmland, water, gold, silver, oil, and so on. (You can read more about these on pages 14–15.)

- Finally, there is the love people have for their land because it's tied to their history, their religion, or both. (This land is yours. And there's no place like home.)

Resources of CONFLICT

Like land, resources have been a source of conflict for thousands of years. WHY?

For starters, having a steady supply of natural resources—ones that come from nature, such as wood or water or minerals—makes a country's citizens feel secure. People like to know that they won't be running out of lumber or oil anytime soon.

In addition, having something that the rest of the world wants also gives a country power. It's kind of like having that awesome snack in your backpack—you can trade it to get other things you want but don't have.

Finally, while some resources—like oil, diamonds, and gold—are valuable because people want them, other resources—like water and food—are vital. People don't just want vital resources, they actually need them to survive.

Re·source:
A vital or valuable asset or natural material, including gold, oil, diamonds, food sources, and money.

So what's the problem?

Conflicts over resources come up for different reasons.

- **It's ours, all ours!** Some conflicts are about who owns or controls the land where the resource is found. These happen less often today than in the past because the borders between most countries are settled. (But conflicts can still come up over the few areas on the planet where borders aren't settled, like some parts of the Arctic.)

- **Hey, you can't cut us off!** Some conflicts over resources are about getting or keeping access to them. For instance, many countries around the world get oil from the handful of nations that have it to sell. When countries feel like their access to that oil is threatened, conflicts arise.

- **Quit hogging all the good stuff!** Some conflicts are about sharing resources, like water, oil, or natural gas, especially when they overlap borders.

- **Money, money, money…** Other conflicts are about who gets the money to be made from selling resources. These disagreements happen most often in countries where there is no real government or the government is dishonest. (See the facing page to read about the so-called resource curse.)

BLUE GOLD

As the world's population grows, more people will need access to fresh water (not the salt water found in oceans and seas). But there's only so much of it to go around. And a lot of industries, including farming and mining and manufacturing, depend on water, too.

With more and more people and industries competing for a limited supply, the price of water will likely go up and up and up. Eventually, water could become too expensive for most people. Many experts think that unless countries reach agreements on how to protect, use, and share the world's supplies, water wars will be part of our future.

WITH TOO LITTLE WATER TO GO AROUND, PEOPLE CAN BECOME DESPERATE. SINCE 2000, WATER SHORTAGES HAVE CONTRIBUTED TO VIOLENT CONFLICTS IN MANY COUNTRIES, INCLUDING YEMEN, SOMALIA, KENYA, AND ETHIOPIA.

A BLESSING or a CURSE?

If natural resources like oil and gold and diamonds are valuable, you'd think that countries with huge amounts of them would be some of the richest in the world. That's true for many countries, including the United States, Canada, Australia, Saudi Arabia, and the United Arab Emirates.

But it's not always the case.

Many countries that are rich in natural resources are still among the poorest in the world. They're also the scenes of some of the most violent conflicts. It's a problem that's known as the resource curse. Angola, the Democratic Republic of the Congo, Liberia, Sierra Leone, and Sudan all suffer from this curse.

Are the resources the problem?

The short answer is no. It's not the resources that make the countries poor or cause their problems. (The resources actually bring a lot of wealth.) Instead, it's dishonest governments—or the lack of any real governments at all—that cause resources to become a curse.

In these cases, the wealth goes into a handful of influential people's pockets instead of enriching the country itself. So a small group of people get rich, while everyone else struggles just to survive.

15

Conflict resources

Con·flict re·source:
A natural resource—such as diamonds, timber, gold, and other minerals—that is traded or sold to help pay for weapons and keep a conflict going.

What do cell phones, laptops, wedding rings, and gasoline have to do with violent conflicts in Africa? They help fuel them. All of these products are made using resources that help pay for armed conflicts in the countries they come from. These resources are known as conflict resources.

Conflict electronics

Imagine a world without computers and cell phones. Impossible? That's why a mineral called coltan is so valuable. It's needed to make just about every kind of electronic gadget there is. Eighty percent of all known coltan is in the Democratic Republic of the Congo (DRC), where violent conflicts have killed millions of people over the past decade. The sale of coltan helps fund the fighting.

The deadly cycle

Conflict resources bring in hundreds of millions or even billions of dollars a year—not for the country but for dishonest government leaders or warlords. They create a deadly cycle that goes like this:

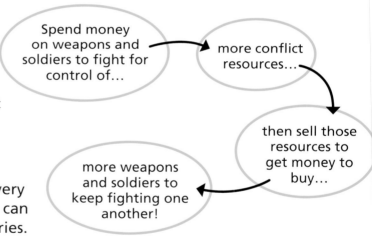

Spend money on weapons and soldiers to fight for control of…

more conflict resources…

then sell those resources to get money to buy…

more weapons and soldiers to keep fighting one another!

Cycles like this are very difficult to stop and can cripple entire countries.

TOUGH TO TRACK

In many places, it's against the law to buy conflict resources, but it can be difficult to tell exactly where resources like diamonds or oil or other minerals come from. People sneak them out of their own countries and sell them in a neighboring nation where they are not conflict resources. From there, the resources make their way to other countries around the world, where they're made into finished products. By the time people buy these goods, there's no way to tell that they were made using conflict resources.

An unFAIR Share

Imagine the most mouth-watering cake ever...except it's being cut by a kid you're not exactly tight with.

You're not surprised when he gives his friends the biggest pieces. Or when he hands the kids he sort of likes decent-sized pieces. And you barely get a sliver.

Now, most of the other kids aren't too worried about your situation—they've got their cake, after all. But how do you feel? And what can you do about it?

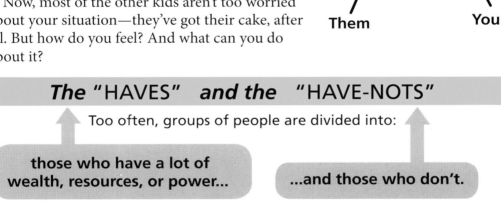

Them   **You**

The "HAVES" and the "HAVE-NOTS"

Too often, groups of people are divided into:

those who have a lot of wealth, resources, or power...

...and those who don't.

These groups can be different countries or groups of people within a country. An idea called conflict theory says that there will always be competition—and conflict—between the haves and the have-nots. Why? Well, there is only so much wealth and power, and so many resources (or cake), to go around. The haves have most of it, and they want to keep it. The have-nots want to get more of it. And that's where the conflict comes in.

Money + Power = Elites

You may not agree with conflict theory, but there's no denying that there are big gaps in the wealth and power people have. These gaps are called inequalities.

Some inequalities are economic—that's how much money people have. Others are social—meaning there are differences in how much power various groups have, what kinds of opportunities they get, and how well they're treated. And within every country, there are also inequalities between the people at the top—the ELITES—and those at the BOTTOM.
How do the people at the bottom feel about this? Usually, not too satisfied.

E·lites:
People considered to be the top of their society because of their wealth and power.

NO SOCIAL JUSTICE?
NO PEACE!

The way people are treated within their society—the fairness that they experience—is called social justice. A country's systems—things like taxes, laws, and schools—play a big part in social justice. The more fair these systems are, the more equal everyone's slice of cake is. How does that work exactly?

The amount of money people earn (called their income) generally depends on their job, which in turn usually depends on their level of education. But school and work are not always easy things to get. In countries without strong social justice, people's race, background, gender, or religion can make it very difficult for them to get the education or job they want—in some places, certain people simply aren't allowed to have either.

DOES POVERTY
CAUSE CONFLICTS?

A lot of armed conflicts happen in very poor countries where people find it tough to get the basic things they need, like food, water, and shelter. This can make it seem like poverty causes violent conflicts. But most experts think it's not that simple. Countries that have extreme poverty and armed conflicts also tend to have governments too weak to keep order. And there are usually few options—like fair laws or courts—for people to settle conflicts peacefully. (For more on this, see chapter 3.)

Don't leave me behind

When people feel as if their country has no social justice, it usually leads to frustration, resentment, and anger. That's especially true when they have the sense that the rich are always getting richer while the poor are left behind. In the right (or wrong) circumstances, those feelings can lead to violent conflicts.

This calls for a revolution!

The gap between rich and poor, powerful and powerless, has helped spark more than one revolution in the past, including the American Revolution (1775–83) and the French Revolution (1789–99). These uprisings led to the end of monarchies (the rule of kings and queens) in the American Colonies (which became the United States) and France.

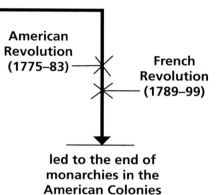

American Revolution (1775–83)

French Revolution (1789–99)

led to the end of monarchies in the American Colonies and France.

Who has control over the way a country is run?

Finally! After a whole year of raising money with your classmates by washing cars, it's time to decide what to spend all that hard-earned cash on. But how should it be spent? And who should make that call?

Countries have governments to make decisions like this (for the country, not for your classroom!). Governments choose where a country's money goes. They also make the laws and pay for the police officers, soldiers, and courts that enforce them. And that's just the start. It's a lot of power.

Who's got the power?

In democracies, people vote to elect the governments they most believe will make good decisions on their behalf. The idea is to give each voter a little bit of power, so that the government answers to the people. When people dislike their government, they can elect a new one. But not all countries are democracies.

No choice, no voice

Some countries don't bother with elections at all. These countries are called dictatorships. Leaders simply put themselves in charge and use the army and the police to make sure they stay there.

Other countries look like democracies and call themselves democracies—even holding elections—but they are really fake democracies. The leaders make sure the elections turn out in their favor by paying people to vote for them, scaring off competitors, or keeping people from voting altogether, known as rigging an election.

> Sometimes, even when they don't manage to win, they lie and claim they did anyway.

Power corrupts? Absolutely!

In a fake democracy or a dictatorship, the government's main goal is to keep itself in power.

This often ends up creating a regime, which is an especially controlling government. Regimes are usually made up of people the leaders trust, like family members, friends, and those they can control through dishonest maneuvers known as corruption. A country's elites, police, and army are also often part of a regime. These people get enough wealth and power to keep them happy.

CAN A GOVERNMENT IN A TRUE DEMOCRACY BE CORRUPT, TOO?

YES, but since democracies have elections every four years or so, it's a lot more difficult for them to control armies, courts, or police the way a long-standing regime can.

To keep everyone else in line, regimes use repression. Sometimes this means using guns and fear to make sure no one challenges them. They can also restrict people's freedoms with laws, making it illegal to speak out against the government, for example, or to meet in large groups (which are needed to plan action or stage protests).

People who have a problem with a country's regime don't have a lot of options for changing it. The laws are not on their side, and neither are the police and the army. They often have to remove the regime by force, and for that, they have three main options.

1 Revolution	2 Coup	3 Invasion
The citizens get so fed up, they rise up and fight to overthrow the government. This is also known as an insurgency or uprising.	The people running the military turn on the leader of the government, take over the country, and make the head of the army the new ruler. (And usually things don't get much better for ordinary citizens.)	Other nations decide that a regime needs to go and invade the country. Countries might invade because the regime is threatening international peace, cutting off access to a valuable resource, or doing awful things to its citizens.

INFORMATION IS POWER

Censorship is a powerful tool of repression. A regime will control newspapers and TV stations, and only allow information that makes its rule look good. Censorship was a lot easier before the internet. Today, anyone with a cell phone can spread information. People can upload and share pictures, videos, and ideas across a country or around the world in seconds. And that's no small thing. In 2010 and 2011, social media played a big part in bringing down regimes throughout the Middle East. People who were fed up with living in dictatorships used social media to organize protests and let the rest of the world know what was happening.

" **Knowledge is power. Information is liberating.** "

—*Kofi Annan, Secretary-General of the United Nations (1938–present)*

chapter 2

People fail to get along because they fear each other; they fear each other because they don't know each other; they don't know each other because they have not communicated with each other.

—Martin Luther King, Jr., leader of African American civil rights movement (1929–68)

DIVIDING LINES

Global conflicts don't turn violent just because two groups want or need the same thing.

After all, groups have disagreements every day of the week: over how to reduce air pollution, how to fund schools, or how to spend tax money. But they don't call each other the "enemy" and start shooting right away.

So how do people get to that point? It's an important thing to figure out, since the way people see each other makes a big difference in how they handle a conflict.

When two sides in a disagreement feel like there's some common ground between them, they're way more likely to talk things out. Each side feels that the other is willing to listen and will be able to understand where they're coming from.

But when the two sides see only their differences, they're more likely to mistrust, fear, and even hate each other. Sometimes one side views the other as an open threat. When that happens, each side ends up seeing the other as an enemy who must be beaten at all costs.

The phrase "making enemies" says a lot. Enemies don't just happen. They are made. The first step in that process is drawing a line between "us" and "them." In the past, the dividing lines were often the actual borders between two countries. But most conflicts today involve groups of people within the same country, and usually they're based on differences in things like religion or ethnic background.

The TIES That BOND *(and Bind)*

Forming groups is part of human nature. It gives people a warm, fuzzy feeling to be part of something.

When people feel good about their group—whether that group is based on culture or religion or country—it can be an important part of their identity. And the pride and sense of unity they feel together can help them accomplish great things.

Sometimes people knowingly become part of a group—by joining a sports team, for example, or a political party—and sometimes they're born into one. Other times, people sort of fall into a group without even thinking about it, because of things they like or don't like.

Who are you?

If someone asked you that question, you'd probably start by saying your name. But then what? How else do you define yourself? Are you smart or funny? Shy or loud? Do you love reading, sports, music, fashion, video games—or all of the above? These traits are part of your unique personal identity.

But you also have a group identity. Do you go to a particular school? Are you part of a team? Do you belong to a church or a mosque or a synagogue? What's your nationality? Are you a skate punk or a goth, a geek or a jock, or none of the above?

Like everyone else on the planet, you define yourself by the groups you belong to. But here's the kicker: you also define yourself by the groups you don't belong to. Deciding what you're not can be just as big a part of your identity as deciding what you are.

Do people just naturally discriminate?

If you had the chance to give a pizza party to either your friends or another groups of kids, who would you choose? Pretty easy, right? Now, what if someone asked you to choose between two groups of kids you've never met and never will? Would you care who got invited to the party? Probably not, right?

Not so fast...

Loose bonds still bind

In 1979, two psychologists brought several teenage boys into a room one by one and asked them to look at two paintings. Based on which painting they said they liked better, the boys were assigned to one of two groups.

Next, the boys were asked to divide pretend money between the two groups in whatever amounts they saw fit. They had no idea who was in their group—since they'd never even seen the other volunteers—but every last boy gave more money to his own group than he did to the other. That might not have been surprising if the boys got a share of the money they were dividing. But they didn't.

My group is better than your group

Psychologists believe this experiment (and others like it) show that:

Dis·crim·i·nate:
To make or see differences; to treat people unfairly based on these differences.

Sta·tus:
Rank or position in society compared to other people or groups.

We will form groups based on just about anything; we have a need to be part of a group, regardless of what that group is.

Once we have a group—even if it's just people who like the same painting we do—we want it to come out on top. **WHY?** Because it's our group. Since we define ourselves by the group to which we belong, our group's status reflects on us. When our group succeeds, we feel better about ourselves.

US VS. THEM

The bad side of the groups we make

Feeling good about the groups we belong to can be a very positive thing. But groups can also bring out the worst in people, especially when they start to focus on the differences between themselves and others.

This focus on differences can lead to "us" and "them" thinking, which in turn can lead to mistrust, stereotyping, prejudice, and even hatred. And when those types of negative emotions are part of a conflict, the odds of people working things out peacefully drop. In fact, most intractable conflicts—the kind that seem to go on forever without any hope of being settled—involve this kind of thinking.

Old habits die hard

Ste·re·o·type:
A simplified assumption that all members of a group are a certain way.

Have you ever felt that a grown-up judged you unfairly just because you were a kid? Maybe someone followed you around a store because she thought you would try to shoplift or another person shooed you and your friends away from a park because he assumed you were up to no good.

That kind of thinking, called stereotyping, is what keeps people apart. The people in one group make up their minds about those in a whole other group—"they're all crooks" or "they're all liars"—without ever really getting to know them.

But that happened fifty years ago!

Prej·u·dice:
A preconceived opinion about a person or group that is usually negative and is based on beliefs instead of facts.

In a lot of cases, the ideas behind stereotypes get passed down from one generation to the next, without anyone really questioning where they came from or what proof there is for them. Sometimes the bad feelings can go back to events that happened ten, fifty, a hundred, or even a thousand years ago!

People stubbornly hold on to their stereotypes because they "know" they are "true." In the end, these ideas are an example of prejudice, and they can make it very difficult to resolve a conflict.

Open minds can do the impossible

Stereotypes aren't impossible to overcome. People just have to be willing to see past their old ways of thinking.

When Israel was created in 1948, it was against the wishes of the countries around it. For more than thirty years, Israel and nearby Egypt were almost constantly at war. The two countries represented two groups with deep mistrust and hatred for one another: Jews and Arabs.

Few believed that peace was possible between these sworn enemies. And yet, in 1979, after months of intense negotiating, Egypt's president Anwar Sadat and Israel's prime minister Menachem Begin signed a peace deal. What did it take for them to get that point? Each one had to believe the other was open to seeing things from his side. Both men also had to be open to compromise and have the courage to stand up to those who were not excited about a peace agreement. And maybe most important, each had to get past long-held stereotypes about the other's intentions.

In the years since this deal, the countries have been peaceful, if not always friendly, neighbors. Today new leaders, who don't share the same views as Sadat and Begin, might break the peace. But nothing can break the example those two leaders set by agreeing to be open to possibilities. Together they called off the state of war that had lasted for decades.

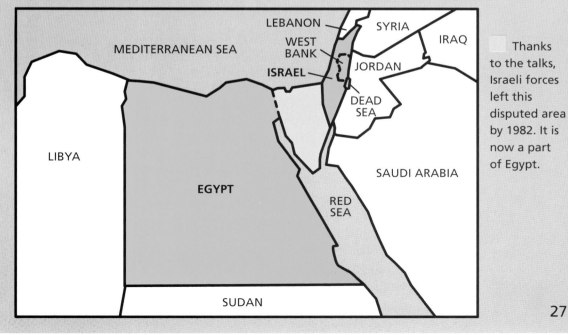

Thanks to the talks, Israeli forces left this disputed area by 1982. It is now a part of Egypt.

Culture CLASHES

Like any other group, an ethnic group can be a huge part of someone's identity.

People in an ethnic group share a history, a culture, a language, and traditions. Often, they feel connected to the group's homeland, too, even if they weren't actually born in that place.

When fighting breaks out between two ethnic groups, it looks like it's all about their differences. The two groups just despise each other so much that they feel the need to destroy each other.

Is it that simple? No way.

There's no denying that the hatred between different groups is very real, and it is part of what leads to ethnic conflicts. But it's not the only problem. Think about it: if two groups of people hate each other so much that they just can't help killing each other, then they should be in violent conflict everywhere they come in contact, right? But that's just not the case.

SAME GROUPS.

DIFFERENT CIRCUMSTANCES.

DIFFERENT OUTCOMES.

Jewish and Arabic people, Serbian and Croatian people, and other groups who've been in armed conflicts in one part of the world can and do peacefully share neighborhoods elsewhere.

Context is key

Why can different groups get along well in some places but not others? Context—what's going on around them—plays a big part.

Hu·man rights: Basic rights that every person has, including the rights to freedom, equality, education, and security; these rights are not respected in every country, though.

Countries where ethnic groups tend to get along have human rights protections, courts, and other institutions for settling disputes, and strong laws that get enforced fairly. Places where ethnic conflicts break out more often lack these things. In these countries, there are usually huge gaps in the wealth and power of different groups, and few protections for those who are discriminated against because of their language, background, or race. When people are treated unfairly—or openly attacked—they don't always have the option of filing a complaint or going to court to try to change things. They feel they must defend themselves, because their society isn't doing it for them (or at least not very well).

28

What causes ethnic conflicts?

It's not so much the actual differences between groups that cause conflicts. It's the "us" and "them" feelings that add fuel to the fire when times get tough and tensions rise. If people in group A are finding it hard to get work but people in group B are getting good jobs, it's probably going to lead to conflict. And that conflict isn't about the two groups speaking different languages or looking dissimilar. It's about how they're treated—the opportunities they have—because of those differences.

At their roots, ethnic conflicts are about the same things as other armed conflicts: power, land, resources, and equality.

ETHNIC CONFLICTS FLARE UP MOST OFTEN WHEN TIMES ARE TOUGH—WHEN **FOOD, WATER,** OR **OTHER RESOURCES** ARE SCARCE.

Then why are they called "ethnic conflicts"?

Good question. Some experts really dislike the term "ethnic conflicts" because they don't think it's accurate—it just talks about the people who are fighting, not what they're actually fighting about. In fact, it's usually people outside a dispute who label it as ethnic. The people who are in the thick of it often say they're fighting for something else, like their rights or their land or the freedom to have a say in how their government operates.

BATTLES OVER BELIEFS

What's behind conflicts over religions? Do they have to happen?

Religion is a huge part of some people's identities—it shapes their beliefs, values, morals, customs, way of life…even what happens after they die. That can make religious beliefs a very tough area of compromise. Each religion has a view of what life is about, how people should live, and what happens when we die. When people feel as if they're being prevented from living the way their religion instructs them to, it often doesn't take long for conflict to arise.

29

Live and let live

People can find ways to accept each other's beliefs and practices. In the United States, the First Amendment to the Constitution guarantees that people can follow the religion of their choice. In Canada, the Charter of Rights and Freedoms ensures the same.

Those guarantees mean that people are free to dress, pray, and live the way their religions say they should. So they can't, for example, be fired from a job or kept out of school because they need to pray several times a day.

When laws or societal values make it tough—if not impossible—for people to practice their religion, countries with religious freedom look for ways to accommodate the differences. Conflicts are usually settled through discussions, debates, and legal reforms.

THE KIRPAN COMPROMISE

When Gurbaj Singh Multani was twelve years old, he was banned from wearing a religious symbol at his school in Montreal, Canada. The symbol was a kirpan, a ceremonial dagger that orthodox Sikh boys and men must wear at all times. Officials at Gurbaj's school felt that the dagger was a threat to the safety of other students. He was faced with the choice of going to school or practicing his religion.

Gurbaj's parents felt that the school's ban went against the Charter of Rights and Freedoms, so they filed a lawsuit. Eventually, the Supreme Court of Canada ruled that as long as Gurbaj kept his kirpan in a wooden box, which in turn would be wrapped in fabric and sewn into his clothes, it was not a threat to other kids' safety. The court felt it was a fair compromise that allowed Gurbaj to practice his religion while still protecting the safety of the other students.

Taken to an extreme

Religion can spark violent conflicts when people take their beliefs to an extreme—when they believe that it is their duty to force others to conform to their religious beliefs and way of life. These people are known as extremists. Extremists believe that they need to destroy any and all threats to their religion. They usually go about destroying those threats with violence.

Although extremists exist in every religion, it's important to remember that they do not represent everyone who practices that religion. Extremists may draw a lot of attention to themselves, but they're actually a small percentage of any religion's followers.

Minorities and
MAJORITIES

■ How does everyone's voice get heard?

Every country in the world is made up of different ethnic and religious groups, as well as gender, language, political, and racial groups. Naturally, some of these groups are bigger than others. (What are the odds of there being exactly the same number of men and women in a country?)

The biggest group in a country is called the majority. Smaller groups are minorities. In most countries, the majority has more power. Because the majority has the most people, a country's laws are usually made with this group in mind. Conflicts often build up when minorities feel that the majority is treating them unfairly; limiting their ability to practice their culture or religion or to speak their language; or even threatening their lives.

Can someone be a part of a majority and a minority at the same time? Absolutely. For example, a person might belong to an ethnic majority but also be a member of a religious minority.

Making room for differences

Some countries listen to what all groups want or need. They look for ways to address as many issues as they can without disturbing all their citizens. This is called accommodation. It's how multicultural countries like the United States, Canada, and the United Kingdom try to handle things. (Usually, the civil rights in such countries were won after many long years of protests and struggle by minority groups.)

...Or Not

But other countries simply ignore the problem. Or they believe that minority groups should conform, or become like the majority. Things can get ugly if minority groups feel as if violence is their only option for change. That's when full-on armed conflicts can break out.

Sep·a·ra·tism:

A movement aimed at creating either a brand-new country or more independent government for a minority group currently within a larger country.

Ci·vil War:

A long-standing violent conflict fought between two or more groups within a single country.

A place of their own

Sometimes the problems between the people in a minority group and the rest of their fellow citizens get so bad that the group decides to separate and form a country of its own. The idea of giving up a piece of their country to this group usually doesn't sit well with everyone else, and a conflict builds. This is known as a civil war.

Other times the minority groups want to self-govern, which means they create their own area inside the country where they can make decisions for themselves. This option usually doesn't go over too well with the rest of the country either. The majority worries that if every minority group got to self-govern, there wouldn't be much of a country left.

Worth the effort

Trying to accommodate the wishes of all minority groups in a country can be difficult. Peaceful countries like Canada spend decades trying to help their many ethnic and religious groups feel accepted, but it doesn't make everyone happy all the time. It's worth the effort, though, because when people stop accepting each other as equals, terrible things can happen.

Eliminating ~~ENEMIES~~

When people become driven by anger, hatred, and fear—when "us" and "them" thinking gets out of control—they can stop seeing each other as human beings. And when this happens, people become capable of incredibly awful acts.

Sometimes, groups of people are taken from their homes and sent to live at harsh work camps. Others are deported, or sent out of the country. But the worst act of all is genocide. The Holocaust—the mass murder of six million Jews by the Nazis during the Second World War—is the most well-known example of this.

Do genocides still happen?

After the Holocaust, countries around the world swore they would never let another genocide happen. But in fact, genocides have since taken place in several countries, including Cambodia, Guatemala, Sudan, Bosnia, and Rwanda.

Gen·o·cide:
The planned mass killing of a specific national, religious, or ethnic group with the goal of eliminating that group entirely.

How can they happen?

Genocides are as difficult to explain as they are to accept. They usually start when a leader is looking to blame his country's problems on someone. The obvious target is a minority group, especially one that already has an uneasy relationship with the majority. The leader labels this group a threat to the country and stirs up people's anger and hatred. This doesn't always end in a genocide, of course. But placing blame is the first step.

Why doesn't anyone stop it?

There are no easy answers to this question, but one thing experts point out is that genocides don't happen overnight. They are planned, and they usually unfold slowly. So slowly, in fact, that at first, people living in the country don't always realize what's happening. By the time they do figure out what's going on, they may do nothing to stop it. There are many reasons for this, including:

- People are scared to get involved or feel relieved that they're not the target.

- People feel as if the genocide has nothing to do with them, especially if they're not actively participating in it.

- Some may want to help but think they can't make a difference. Others believe that the situation isn't what it appears to be.

- Some people are caught up in blaming the targeted group and therefore support the killings and don't want the genocide to stop.

The importance of digging deeper

Genocides show what can happen when people see conflicts in the most black and white terms possible. Faced with a problem, they accept that one group is the cause. But just like any other conflict, if you dig a little deeper, you find out pretty quickly that things are never that simple.

The
Deep Roots
of CONFLICT

Dividing lines aren't drawn overnight. Most conflicts have histories that go back decades or even centuries.

The recent war in Afghanistan may look like a brand-new conflict with the Afghan government, the United States, and other NATO (North Atlantic Treaty Organization) countries fighting against the Taliban. But many of these countries and groups have a long history of fighting to control Afghanistan.

Long ago, Afghanistan's location between Asia, India, and the Middle East made it important for trade. Today, its neighbors are major oil and natural gas producers. Afghanistan also has its own newly discovered mineral wealth.

1747 Afghanistan forms

For centuries, the land that is Afghanistan today is conquered by outsiders. For most of this early history, tribes of people who belong to different ethnic groups settle the area. Many of these tribes still exist today.

By 1747 the largest ethnic group is the Pashtuns. The chiefs of Pashtun tribes come together and select a single leader, Ahmad Shur Durrani. He brings people across present-day Afghanistan and Pakistan, as well as parts of Iran and India, under his control.

1933–73
Afghanistan's last king

The 40-year reign of Muhammad Zahir Shah, part of a 200-year rule by Pashtuns, is one of the most peaceful in Afghanistan's history. But although there is peace, there is little prosperity. Some people become frustrated.

1800s The Great Game

The two biggest empires in the world—the United Kingdom (UK) and Russia—fight to control Central Asia. Throughout the 1800s, Russia's moves in and around Afghanistan make the UK nervous, especially since one of the UK's biggest, richest colonies—India— is right next door. The UK launches three separate wars in Afghanistan to try to gain control of the country—or at least weaken Russia's influence. After the Second Anglo-Afghan War, Afghanistan agrees to let the UK control its foreign affairs, or its dealings with other countries. After the Third Anglo-Afghan War, in 1919, Afghanistan gains independence from the UK and becomes friendly with Russia.

1973 Coup

Muhammad Zahir Shah travels to Italy for surgery. While he is away, his cousin, Mohammad Daoud Khan, takes control of the country in a coup. To avoid a war, Zahir abdicates, or gives up, his rule. Still, many are opposed to Daoud being in power.

1978 Saur Revolution

Daoud is killed when the communist People's Democratic Party of Afghanistan (PDPA), overthrows the government. One of the PDPA's leaders, Nur Mohammad Taraki, takes control and suggests making changes that upset a lot of people. Taraki also signs treaties with the Union of Soviet Socialist Republics (USSR).

1979 The USSR invades

With Taraki dead, the USSR worries about losing its influence in Afghanistan, so it invades and puts a new president in place. The Mujahideen fight the new government and the Soviet army. Many countries, including the United States, Pakistan, China, Iran, and Saudi Arabia, support the Mujahideen with money, weapons, and training.

1978
The Mujahideen emerges

Many Muslims feel Taraki's changes threaten their beliefs. In rural areas, groups known as Mujahideen (holy warriors) form to fight the changes. Civil war breaks out. Taraki is killed, and his rival, Hafizullah Amin, names himself leader.

1988 The USSR leaves

Afghanistan, the United States, Pakistan, and the Soviet Union sign an agreement to end the war. A pro-USSR government is in Afghanistan when their soldiers leave.

1992–96
Afghan Civil War

In 1992, the Mujahideen overthrow the government and take control of most of the country. But now leaders within the Mujahideen cannot agree and begin a civil war amongst themselves.

1996
The Northern Alliance emerges

Many groups that were part of the Mujahideen now fight to keep the Taliban out of their territory in the north. They become known as the Northern Alliance.

1994
The Taliban emerges

During the civil war, another group—the Taliban—emerges. By 1996, they control most of the country and declare themselves the official government, but few countries recognize this.

2001 The Taliban falls

After the September 11th attacks, the Taliban offers members of the terrorist group al-Qaeda a place to hide. The United States invades to defeat the Taliban and remove them from power. Allies such as the UK and Canada, as well as the Northern Alliance, join the fight. In December 2001, they take control of the country.

So why didn't the fighting end in 2001?

The Taliban didn't just disappear after being removed from power in 2001—they continued to fight. Soldiers from the United States, United Kingdom, and Canada didn't leave. They and other countries became part of an International Security Assistance Force (ISAF) run by NATO. They stayed in Afghanistan to help the new government keep control. And all the while, in many areas tribes have also been battling amongst themselves.

There's always more to it

Like the many wars through Afghan history, most conflicts are much more complicated than one side versus another. Learning about the history of groups in any conflict can not only help us better understand why they're in conflict today, but it can also show how alliances can change over time.

chapter 3

You can't shake hands with a clenched fist.

—*Indira Gandhi, Prime Minister of India (1917–84)*

Cooperation or COMBAT?

It's not that hard to figure out why conflicts occur and get resolved between people in day-to-day life: two people want the same thing, and they find a way to hash out who gets it.

FACE-TO-FACE

SOMETIMES THEY TALK IT OUT.

SOMETIMES THEY DON'T.

In many ways, countries don't behave all that differently from individual people. When you look at what's happening out there in the big, wide world, it's easy to find examples of conflicts over land, resources, power, ideas, and beliefs that have blown up into bloody wars.

But—and this is an important but—there are also plenty of conflicts that arose over similar issues and didn't end in war. Or even violence. The countries involved found other ways to settle their differences.

So why do some disputes lead to violence while others get settled without it? Maybe understanding why wars don't happen is as important as understanding why they do.

39

Why Countries
GET ALONG :)
:[...or NOT

Imagine you're out shopping with your best friend. You both spot the most amazing T-shirt at the same time. There's only one left, and you both want it. How would you decide who gets it?

Now, what if the person making a grab for the shirt wasn't your best friend but a kid you only sort of knew? Would you handle the conflict differently?

How would you handle things if the other person was a kid who took every chance to make your life miserable? Would you be more or less likely to work it out nicely?

Countries are people, too

The relationships you have with people can affect how you handle conflicts with them. And in much the same way, the relationships between countries have a lot to do with how they handle their conflicts.

SOME COUNTRIES GET ALONG REALLY WELL. OTHERS, NOT SO MUCH.

Countries that have strong, friendly relationships and open lines of communication are more likely to work out their disagreements peacefully than those that don't. That's especially true when the countries have things in common, and even more so when they depend on each other for trade (that's when countries sell goods to each other).

Friends, enemies, and everything in between

Countries, like individual people, generally fall into one of three groups: allies, acquaintances, or enemies.

ALLIES are countries that are like close friends.

They often

- have the same type of government or economy
- speak the same language(s) and have similar values
- trade a lot with one another
- have each other's backs during international disputes

Other countries are **ACQUAINTANCES**—not enemies, but not great friends either. They try to stay friendly, but acquaintances can't be counted on the way allies can.

They often

- have different languages, values, and types of government or economies

But each one also

- has something the other country needs or wants
- wants to avoid making the other angry

Then there are **ENEMIES**—countries that have a hostile relationship.

They often

- have very different types of governments or economies
- speak different languages
- trade very little
- openly argue with and defy each other on big issues

TOO ALIKE TO FIGHT?

If you live in a democratic country, you can bet with almost 100 percent certainty that you will never go to war against another democratic country. Why is that? Experts aren't exactly sure, but they have a few ideas.

- Democratic leaders have to answer to voters, who usually don't want war.

- People living in democracies are used to settling things by talking. That becomes the usual way of handling conflicts outside the country as well.

- Non-democratic countries can seem like more of a threat. Because democracies and non-democracies are so different, misunderstandings are more likely.

WORLD ORDER:
Who Rules the
"SCHOOL"?

Have you ever felt pressure to befriend someone you really don't like all that much just because the rest of the kids in your group have? Have you shied away from hanging out with someone because everyone else thinks he or she is weird… and you're worried they'll all think you're weird, too?

Well, countries can influence friendships much as you and your classmates do.

Welcome to Planet Earth High

Let's pretend the world is like one of those high schools on TV, and the countries are its students. The rich kids have a lot of power. So do the tough ones. When kids are rich and tough, they practically rule the school—they're the superpowers. Many kids want to be friends with the superpowers in the hope that some of their popularity will rub off. At the very least, everyone wants to stay on their good side (whether they like them or not).

Power plays

The amount of power a country has in the world affects how it handles conflicts. Less powerful countries usually think twice about letting a conflict with a more powerful country get out of hand. They'll try to work it out peacefully because they know they're not likely to win a war.

A superpower, on the other hand, knows that it has the strength and money to defeat just about any other country. Very often, it can get what it wants just by asking for it. The fear of landing on the superpower's bad side can intimidate other countries into settling conflicts quickly—or even avoiding them altogether.

Forming "clubs"

If the world is like a high school, then international alliances are kind of like clubs. Countries form alliances because they want to work toward the same interests or goals. Most alliances are either economic or military in nature.

Economic alliances help countries boost trade so they can make more money (sort of like a street-wide garage sale).

Countries in military alliances are more intimidating than countries on their own are (like walking down the hallway with all your friends behind you).

Naturally, when countries in an alliance have conflicts, they are way more likely to settle them peacefully. But an alliance doesn't just affect the way members deal with each other. It also influences the way they act toward countries that aren't part of their club. Countries in an alliance back each other up when it comes to dealing with the rest of the world. When you challenge one alliance member, you're challenging the whole group.

THE COLD WAR

For most of the twentieth century, there were two superpowers in the world: the United States and the USSR, or Soviet Union. They were as different as two countries could be, in their systems of government, economies, languages, and values. Each country was convinced that the other was out to take over the world. To stop the spread of the other's ideology (that's a way of thinking and living), each tried to get as many countries on its side as possible. The resulting conflict, known as the Cold War, affected just about every country on the planet. It finally ended in 1991, when the Soviet Union fell apart.

Cold War allies of the US and USSR

- United States
- US allies
- USSR
- Soviet allies
- Neutral countries

43

Nations UNITED

If you think of the world as a big school, the United Nations (UN) is kind of like the student council.

The United Nations is meant to give countries a voice in the world and a place to sort out their differences peacefully. Through the UN, countries work together to reach goals, settle disputes, and decide on a code of conduct for everyone to follow.

The UN was formed in 1945, after the end of the Second World War—the biggest, bloodiest war ever. No one wanted to see another conflict like it. About fifty countries decided that the best way to prevent a third world war was to agree on some common goals and work on them together—to make a global community so that people would feel connected no matter where they lived.

It's in the Charter

UN members have to agree to follow some basic rules, and these are spelled out in the Charter of the United Nations. Countries promise they'll do everything they can to avoid violence and to work on peaceful solutions to their problems. That doesn't mean they always manage to settle things peacefully. But when conflicts and wars do break out, the UN tries to get the countries involved to stop the fighting and work on a nonviolent solution.

The United Nations

Started: October 24, 1945

Members: 193 countries

Official languages: Arabic, Chinese, English, French, Russian, Spanish

The idea that countries need to work together to settle conflicts peacefully isn't new. In 1795, a philosopher named Immanuel Kant first imagined the countries of the world forming a "league of peace."

What the UN isn't

The United Nations is not the boss of the world.

It doesn't have limitless power to tell countries what to do.

It cannot get involved in conflicts within countries—only between them.

It doesn't listen to just one opinion. Its members must agree on what actions or measures it takes.

The Security Council

The Security Council is a smaller group within the UN in charge of keeping the peace between countries. It keeps an eye on situations around the world and gets involved when it looks like conflicts might be brewing. Countries can also ask the Security Council to step in and help them settle their conflicts.

How the council works—and doesn't

The Security Council first tries to get countries to resolve any conflicts through negotiation, mediation, or arbitration (see pages 46–49). If those methods don't work, the council might impose sanctions (see pages 50–51). As a last resort, it could approve using force.

Who's on the Security Council?

The five countries that won the Second World War—the United States, the United Kingdom, Russia, China, and France—are permanent members. Ten other countries have seats on the council for two years at a time.

NEGOTIATION:
Talking It Out
More than just having a little chat.

When you hear the phrase "global conflict," what pops into your head? Do you picture soldiers with guns blazing and bombs exploding? Or do you picture people in suits sitting around a big table and trying to sort things out? If you picked the first one, it's not surprising.

THE ART OF DIPLOMACY

You've probably noticed in everyday life that talking things out takes some patience. It also takes skill to convince other people to go along with what you want.

Now imagine trying to convince someone who doesn't speak the same language, share the same culture, or have the same goals as you. Not easy, right? That's why countries often use skilled people called diplomats to negotiate for them. Diplomats are highly trained in the art of dealing with people. They also know a lot about other countries, cultures, and languages, and they use this knowledge to hash out agreements.

In a lot of cases, though, countries do work out their disagreements peacefully. That doesn't mean people always remember to use their inside voices (governments are made up of human beings, after all). But it does mean there are options for resolving things before the various sides start grabbing their guns.

Often, the first option is negotiating, or talking it out.

The biggest slice

Negotiations are kind of like trying to divide a pie—everyone wants the biggest piece. Often the goal is to get as much as possible for yourself while giving up as little as possible to someone else. That's hard to do when the person on the other side of the table has the exact same goal.

HOW CAN YOU BOTH GET THE BIGGEST PIECE?

The short answer is you can't. There can be only one biggest piece, and whoever gets it is the winner. That way of seeing a negotiation—as a competition with only one winner—is called a zero-sum game.

Back for more

When a negotiation turns into a zero-sum game, it becomes a lot harder to settle, and it usually doesn't stay settled for long. The side that feels as if it lost is unsatisfied, and it will bring up the conflict again the first chance it gets, in the hopes of winning it this time.

Everybody's a winner

Trying to turn a zero-sum game into a win-win situation is a common goal for diplomats—along with businesspeople, lawyers, teachers, and anyone else who spends their day trying to settle conflicts. (After all, conflicts happen everywhere, every day.)

WHEN BOTH SIDES IN A DISPUTE WALK AWAY FEELING LIKE THEY GAINED SOMETHING, THEY'RE MORE LIKELY TO BE SATISFIED AND THE CONFLICT WILL STAY SETTLED.

MEDIATION AND ARBITRATION

Have you ever been caught in the middle of an argument between two friends? You want them to stop, and deep down, they do, too. But neither one of them wants to give in. They're caught in a zero-sum game. So they ask what you think.

If you help your friends keep talking until they find a solution, you're acting like a mediator. If they ask you to settle the disagreement for them, you're acting like an arbitrator.

Either way, you're outside of the conflict—a third party. It's often a lot easier for a third party to see a win-win solution. People in the conflict often can't see it because they're each too devoted to their causes.

Orange you glad Mom was here?

An old story about an orange does a pretty good job of showing how a mediator can help solve a conflict.

Two sisters were fighting over the last orange in the house. Each one kept grabbing it out of the other's hands, shouting that she wanted it more. Finally, their mom had had enough. She offered to split the orange and give each girl half.

Both sisters refused, saying they needed the whole thing. The mother asked each girl why she couldn't share. It turned out that one wanted to squeeze the orange for juice and the other wanted the peel to make perfume.

So even though both kids had insisted they wanted the whole orange, it turns out they each really wanted only part of it. By finding out why they wanted the orange, their mom acted like a mediator and helped the girls see that they could both have what they wanted. It became a win-win situation.

Can you just figure it out for us?

But sometimes negotiation and mediation just don't work. The two sides can't agree, even with a mediator's help. In those situations, countries sometimes use arbitration to settle their disagreements. Arbitrators are kind of like judges. They listen to both sides of a conflict and then decide how to settle it. What they say goes.

Me·di·a·tion:
A method for settling a conflict in which an impartial person works with all sides to reach an agreement.

Ar·bi·tra·tion:
A method for settling a conflict in which all sides make their case and an impartial person decides how it will be settled.

48

Long (camel) division

There's an old Islamic fable that shows how helpful an arbitrator can be.

Three brothers were left with seventeen camels when their father died. The oldest son was to have half of them, the middle son one-third of them, and the youngest son one-ninth.

"How can we divide seventeen by half?" the brothers wondered. *"It just doesn't work."*

None of the brothers could take his camels until all three agreed on the numbers. They became frustrated and angry. Finally, they decided to let the village wisewoman divide the camels for them.

She thought about it for a while, then said, *"I'll give you one of my camels. That will make eighteen, which you can divide in half."*

So the oldest son took his half—nine camels—and the middle son took his third—six camels—and the youngest son took his ninth—two camels. But then they realized that they had one camel left over.

(You do the math: 9 + 6 + 2 = 17.)

"Can I have my camel back now?" the wisewoman asked.

It turns out that the solution to their problem was there all along; they just couldn't see it!

17 camels ÷ 3 sons
son 1 - 1/2
son 2 - 1/3
son 3 - 1/9

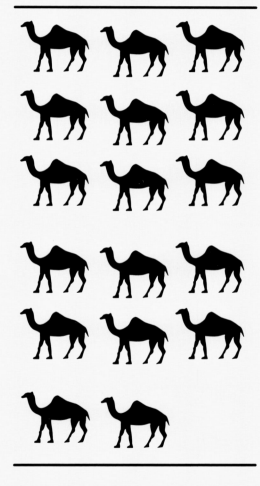

SANCTIONS:
Putting On Some **Pressure**

What if someone was spreading rumors about you behind your back? What could you do to get him to stop?

You could try giving him the cold shoulder. But since he probably doesn't like you anyway, it really wouldn't bother him if you ignored him.

But what if you could convince everyone else in your class to ignore him? That might get his attention! After a week or two of being completely shut out, he might start to think twice about bad-mouthing you.

Sanctions between countries

Sanc·tion: A penalty for breaking a rule or law.

That's kind of how sanctions work. Several nations get together and put pressure on an aggressive country to try to convince it to change its behavior. Sanctions are used most often against countries that are

- using or threatening to use violence against their own people
- creating or buying weapons the world doesn't think they should have
- picking fights with their neighbors

COUNTRIES CAN IMPOSE, OR USE, DIPLOMATIC, ECONOMIC, OR MILITARY SANCTIONS.

1. Diplomatic sanctions

Diplomatic sanctions are kind of like giving a country the cold shoulder. Governments may cancel official visits, remove their diplomats, or ask that country's diplomats to leave their nation. These sanctions are meant to shame the country in front of the rest of the world.

2. Economic sanctions

Economic sanctions may include blocking money from going into the country and blocking the flow of goods. Although they're meant to make life tough for the government, economic sanctions can sometimes make life tough for everyone else in the country instead. The leaders of these governments often have money secretly stashed in banks around the world, so they can keep on living comfortably while everyone else feels the pinch. As a result, economic sanctions don't always change the nation's behavior.

3. Military sanctions

Military sanctions are meant to weaken a country so it loses any appetite it may have had for war. They include blocking shipments of weapons—or anything that could be used as weapons—and even destroying the country's arms factories, missile launchers, and other military targets.

A last resort

Economic and military sanctions are usually the last chance to avoid using force against a country. Sometimes just the threat of economic or military sanctions can convince a country to behave better, and the conflict gets resolved. But sometimes, the country ignores the threat and goes on misbehaving. Once sanctions are imposed, they often stay in place for years—or until an all-out war breaks out.

From BUILDUP to BLOWUP In conflicts, the stakes can get raised fast.

Experts who spend their time trying to figure out conflicts don't always see them the same way, but they do agree on one thing: it's easier to resolve conflicts earlier than later.

Another thing the experts agree on is that there's usually some sort of escalation, or buildup, before conflicts turn violent. Depending on what goes on during that buildup, a conflict can get settled peacefully or explode into violence.

Talks versus tanks

For conflicts to get resolved peacefully, all the sides involved have to be on the same page about a few important points.

They must want to

avoid a bloody, expensive war

+

be seen in a good light by the rest of the world

+

set aside emotions and think logically about solutions to the conflict

But the sides in a conflict aren't always on the same page.

Sometimes one side weighs the costs of war—not only the lives and dollars it will cost, but also its reputation—against what it hopes to gain and decides that it's worth it.

Sometimes one side is just not interested in working things out. It wants all or nothing—and the only way it can get what it wants is to take it by force. The other side doesn't have much choice but to fight back.

When one side mistrusts the other, it's easy to misunderstand an action or a comment. The misunderstanding can have one side assuming the worst—that the other side is threatening its survival. At this point, it doesn't take much to start violence.

Pulling the "trigger"

When conflicts do get violent, people often look back later and see that a specific event, called a trigger, set things off. It's easy to think that this was the actual cause of the conflict. But if you think about a conflict like a gun, there's more to firing it than just pulling the trigger. Loading a gun is like the buildup that happens in every conflict. If the gun isn't loaded, pulling the trigger won't do anything.

This little piggy almost triggered a war

On June 15, 1859, a pig wandered into a potato garden and nearly set off a war. It happened on a small island off the coast of British Columbia and Washington State. British ranchers and American farmers had been living there for years, but they didn't like or trust each other.

So what does the pig have to do with anything? It belonged to a British rancher and was shot by an American farmer who was trying to protect his potatoes. The rancher complained to British soldiers, and the soldiers threatened to arrest the American if he didn't fork over some serious dough for the pork.

But the Americans weren't about to let British soldiers push them around on "their" island, so they sent in some soldiers of their own. For more than a month, tensions rose on the tiny island. Finally, the British governor ordered an attack, but his commander refused to follow through. He thought it was ridiculous to go to war over a pig. His cool head prevailed, and the higher-ups on both sides had no choice but to work out a deal to share the island.

Is War UNAVOIDABLE?

" Mankind must put an end to war before war puts an end to mankind. "

—*John F. Kennedy, U.S. President (1917–63)*

" I'm not so naive or simplistic to believe we can eliminate war. "

—*Robert McNamara, U.S. Secretary of Defense (1916–2009)*

If you gave people three wishes, world peace would probably appear somewhere on most lists. War is violent and destructive, and most people would agree with John F. Kennedy's take on things: we'd be better off without it.

But at the same time, a lot of people would also agree with Robert McNamara. Even though they wish peace could exist, they don't really believe we can get rid of war completely.

Is McNamara right? Is war something we just can't escape? Or is it only conflict that is unavoidable?

Are people made to fight?

Some people believe that war is just part of human nature. But is it? A group of twenty scientists from around the world didn't think so. In 1986, they wrote the Seville Statement on Violence, which says there's **NO scientific proof that**

- people are violent because our ancestors were

- war or any other violent behavior is programmed into human DNA

- evolution favors aggressive behavior

- human beings have a "violent brain"

- war is caused by "instinct" or any single reason

The Seville Statement ends by saying, "The same species who invented war is capable of inventing peace. The responsibility lies with each of us."

Defusing conflict

Many countries have worked together to create a system for resolving their conflicts peacefully (or at least trying to). This system includes things like international laws and courts, and organizations like the United Nations. Many countries also have their own systems for resolving conflicts inside their borders. When people are unhappy with the way things are, they have options: they can go on strike, protest in the streets, or go through the courts to try to make changes to laws. More often than not, disputes in these countries tend to get settled without using violence.

No way to defuse tensions

But in many parts of the world, people simply do not have those options. Sometimes there are no systems in place to allow citizens to work out their differences. They are not allowed to protest, and the courts are not set up fairly. And when people have no other choice, they often use violence to settle their disagreements.

Yet even in such places, peaceful progress is possible. Some of the biggest—and seemingly least resolvable—conflicts in recent history have been settled without violence.

Father of a nation

Mahatma Gandhi led India's fight for independence from the UK from the 1920s to the 1940s. Gandhi's fight was based on non-cooperation. Through boycotts and a refusal to pay taxes, Indians made it very difficult for the British to control the country.

His dream came true

In the United States in the 1960s, Martin Luther King, Jr., followed Gandhi's example, using nonviolent protests such as sit-ins and marches in the African-American fight for civil rights.

From prisoner to president

Nelson Mandela also used peaceful means in the fight to end apartheid in South Africa—although not always. Mandela spent 27 years in prison for his part in violence against the government. While he was there, he became the face of the fight to end apartheid. When he was released in 1990, Mandela continued his work. He was honest about the possibility of violence but first chose to try negotiating with South Africa's president, F. W. de Klerk. The negotiations were a success, and in 1993, he and de Klerk won the Nobel Peace Prize. In 1994, Mandela was elected the president of South Africa.

chapter 4

We must wage peace as vigilantly as we wage war.

—The Dalai Lama, head monk of Tibetan Buddhism (1950–present)

Making PEACE

A famous proverb says,

" History is written by the victors. "

It's basically a way of saying that whoever wins a fight gets to tell what happened—the winner's side of the story is the only one that gets told.

But this proverb kind of makes it sound like history is just one long fight. What happened to the stories of people working out their conflicts and finding ways to get along? After all, peace has been part of human history just as long as war has.

Words and symbols for peace have shown up on everything from ancient scrolls and tablets to tomb walls.

There is a word for "peace" in most age-old languages, from Greek (*eirene*) and Latin (*pax*) to Arabic (*salam*) and Hebrew (*shalom*).

People not only have different words for peace, they have different ideas of what peace is. Some would say it's just a calm period that breaks out between wars and armed conflicts, while others would insist there's more to it than that. To them, peace is not just the opposite or absence of war. They believe that peace is something people build. It is the harmony that comes from people working together, respecting each other, and treating others fairly.

So what, exactly, is peace to you?

From WAR to WORDS:
How Do Armed Conflicts End?

There are basically three ways for wars and armed conflicts to end.

1 **One side** realizes that it doesn't have the money, the soldiers, the weapons, or the desire for more fighting. It surrenders, or gives up. One side clearly wins and the other clearly loses.

2 **Both sides** realize that they're never going to beat each other, and they agree to stop fighting. No one wins and no one loses. That's known as a draw.

3 **Neither side** is willing to give up, so a third party—someone who's not part of the fight—tries to convince both sides to work it out.

The way a conflict ends has a lot to do with the peace process, or how peace gets made.

Peace pro·cess: Negotiations, mediations, and other steps taken to end an armed conflict and reach a peace agreement.

Clear winner

In the past, most wars ended when one side could no longer carry on. There was a clear winner and a clear loser, and the loser didn't have much say in what happened once the guns stopped firing.

The peace process involved the winner making decisions and telling the loser how it was going to be from that point on. Usually, the winner drew new borders and demanded reparations, or money to repay the costs of the war. Sometimes the winner just went ahead and took over the loser's territory.

No clear winner

Since the end of the Second World War in 1945, however, fewer wars have ended that way. It's become more common for armed conflicts to conclude in a draw of some kind. When wars end this way, the peace process is very different. Both sides have to reach an agreement about how to move forward without fighting. In most cases, that makes getting to peace a lot more complicated.

PEACE Processes ☑

"War is hell,"

said William Tecumseh Sherman, a famous American Civil War general, and no one's ever really disagreed with him. But if wars make people miserable, why is it so hard to stop the fighting?

Trust is a big part of keeping peace—both sides have to believe that they won't get attacked the second they let down their guard. That kind of trust is not always easy to find in a war zone.

Put down your weapons!

Peace brokers can convince both sides to set down their weapons and try to work out an agreement. A peace broker is a third party—usually another country or the UN—that has no interest in seeing either side come out on top. If one side suspects that a peace broker favors the other side, there's no way it will agree to stop fighting and talk things out.

Bro·ker: Someone who helps make a deal happen between others; a go-between.

A break in the fighting

Anytime the sides in an armed conflict agree to take a break from fighting, it's called a ceasefire. Ceasefires can be really short—less than a day—or they can go on for months or even years.

Sides might agree to a short ceasefire to let humanitarian workers come into certain areas and help ordinary people who are being hurt by the fighting. As soon as the ceasefire is up, the workers leave and the two sides go back to their fight.

When both sides are open to peace talks, they usually agree to a longer ceasefire. In wars that have a lot of sides or involve groups that aren't official armies, it can be tough to get everyone on board. But if everyone can agree, it's the first step to ending the conflict.

Peace talk

During a ceasefire, brokers work with both sides to open up peace talks. They may act as go-betweens, carrying messages from one side to the other; bring leaders from both sides together to talk face-to-face; or act as mediators, searching for a deal all parties can live with. Most important, peace brokers try to keep everyone at the table when the sides are thinking of giving up on the talks.

Peace promises

Getting both sides to agree to stop fighting for good is no easy thing. It can take years to work out a peace agreement that both sides are willing to sign. A peace agreement is kind of like a contract. It says what each side is willing to give up, do, or not do to keep the peace in the future.

To reach an agreement, both sides in a conflict have to see eye to eye on what it was about in the first place. What are the major issues they want to have settled in the peace agreement? Just getting them to agree on that can take a long time. Sometimes, it never happens, and the peace talks fall apart.

But it's far from hopeless—since 1990, more than six hundred peace agreements have been signed around the world.

Keeping the PEACE

When fighting stops, the peace that follows can be pretty fragile.

People are tense and scared, and they still don't really trust those on the other side. It wouldn't take much for fighting to break out all over again. One of the best ways to keep that from happening is to make sure that the sides in a conflict stay out of each other's way until things cool down.

Peace police

Peacekeepers are soldiers who help with that. Usually, peacekeepers work on behalf of the United Nations. The UN doesn't have its own army, though—it asks its member nations to send soldiers to serve under UN control. Peacekeepers get involved only when all the parties to a conflict agree to it.

Keeping the sides apart

Peacekeepers often go into countries at the start of peace talks. Their job is to keep the sides apart during a ceasefire. They make sure no one crosses a line or picks up weapons, restarting the conflict. They keep things as calm as possible.

Creating calm

Peacekeepers also go into countries where things are unstable. Countries become unstable when there's no rule of law—that means no real government, police force, or system for keeping people in check. This situation often happens right after a government gets overthrown. Violence can break out at any moment in these unstable countries, especially when different groups are trying to take power for themselves. Peacekeepers try to keep that from happening so elections for a new government can be held.

Mission impossible (sometimes)

Peacekeepers face a tough job. There are usually so few of them compared to the number of people they're supposed to protect. They have guns, but they're only allowed to use them in self-defense or to protect ordinary people from harm.

Not every country in the UN pays the costs of peacekeeping missions. A few countries pay most of the expenses—and supply most of the soldiers. When those countries reach the limit of what they can give, there may not be as many peacekeepers as there should be, and they may not have all the equipment they need. That can make it tough to keep armed enemies from going back to battle again.

Lester B. Pearson, Canada's prime minister from 1963 to 1968, suggested the first UN peacekeeping mission in 1956, to help settle the Suez Crisis, a conflict between Egypt and Israel, the United Kingdom, and France.

61

Making
PEACE *Last*

Completing peace talks is a big step, but it's only the first one in a pretty long journey.

The rest of that journey is called peace building. This is a process that involves both sides in a conflict, as well as other groups or nations that want to help them work things out. Peace building is the name for all the meetings, plans, and agreements that try to fix the problems that led to a conflict in the first place. And it's important, because if these problems don't get solved—in a way everyone can live with—peace won't last. As soon as the peacekeepers leave—and sometimes even before that—fighting will break out again.

Making things more fair

Most violent conflicts today are between people living in the same country. These people feel they have an unfair share of power, resources, land, wealth, or some combination of these things.

The goal of peace building is to give citizens a fair say in their country, to make sure they are respected, and to offer them peaceful options for settling their conflicts.

PEACE BUILDING CAN INCLUDE

- reaching agreements about all the changes that need to happen
- setting up fair, honest elections in which everyone can vote
- helping soldiers return to their communities and regular life
- improving people's standard of living
- reconstructing roads and buildings that were destroyed in the conflict
- passing laws and training new police officers
- building a legal system that protects and respects human rights

Building a future together (patiently…)

Peace building depends on creating a feeling of trust between the two sides in a conflict. It depends on bringing people together and getting everyone to see a future where they have opportunities and can imagine working toward common goals.

That doesn't happen overnight, or in a week, or even in a month. It can take years—even decades—to completely settle conflicts and create the right conditions for peace. In the end, trying to get people to be patient and hold on to hope can be one of the biggest challenges in building peace.

Stan·dard of liv·ing: The level of wealth and comfort people have in areas such as housing, education, health care, and food.

The Robbers Cave experiment

What happens when groups in conflict have to work toward a common goal? That's what a psychologist named Muzafer Sherif wanted to find out.

Sherif set up a fake summer camp in Robbers Cave State Park in Oklahoma for eleven- and twelve-year-old boys. Before the twenty-two boys left for the camp, they were randomly divided into two groups. For the first week, each group spent time bonding. The boys named their groups and made flags and shirts, but neither group knew about the other.

The second week, the groups came face to face to compete in games. As the competition heated up, so did the tension. The boys called each other names and almost came to blows. It wasn't long before the two groups refused to have anything to do with each other.

Sherif wanted to see what it would take to get the boys to sort out their differences. They watched a movie and some fireworks together, but nothing improved. Then the camp's water pipe was damaged, and the boys were asked to fix it. Suddenly they all had the same goal. After a few days of working together, they were getting along just fine!

chapter 5

It is not our **differences** that **divide us.** It is our **inability** to **recognize,** **accept,** and **celebrate** those **differences.**

—*Audre Lorde, Caribbean-American writer and activist (1934–92)*

Making Sense of CONFLICTS

Making sense of a global conflict can be kind of like trying to put together a thousand-piece jigsaw puzzle without looking at the picture on the box.

You see little pieces of the big picture, but it's really hard to figure out how they fit together. To make matters more difficult, the pieces you need don't come in a handy little package. You have to ask a lot of questions to find them.

Who is fighting?

Who are the groups involved?

How do they see themselves?

How do they see each other?

What's the history between them?
This is a biggie—a lot of conflicts happening today have their roots in things that happened fifty, a hundred, or even thousands of years ago. Could that still be adding fuel to the fire now?

What are they fighting about?
Remember, there's usually more than one thing at stake. Two groups may seem to be fighting about which one gets to use a river, but there's probably more to it. Is it just a way for one group to have power over the other?

What do the two sides want?
What they want is not the same as what they say they want. Remember the girls with the orange? They both said they wanted the whole orange, but each one actually wanted only part of it (page 48).

Who else is involved?
Have any third-party countries, groups, or organizations weighed in? Are they threatening to get involved? Or are they trying to push for peace?

Why are they involved?
Do they simply want to see the fighting end? Or do they have something to gain from seeing one side win or lose?

**In·formed
o·pin·ion:**
A view or
judgment of
something that
is based on facts,
solid information,
or firsthand
knowledge.

And why would you want to know all this stuff?

Asking lots of questions, knowing where to find the answers, and being able to make sense of them is a pretty powerful skill. It means you'll never have to take someone else's word for what's going on. You'll know how to have an informed opinion of your own.

You can become the most powerful kind of global citizen there is—a knowledgeable one.

Looking for ANSWERS ???

There are a lot of places you can go to find the answers you need to figure out what you think about a conflict. You can search online for articles and blogs, grab books from the library, watch news reports or read newsmagazines, and talk with other people and weigh their opinions.

Facts and opinions

As you're looking at all those videos and articles, it's important to remember that facts and opinions aren't the same thing.

- **Facts** are statements that are 100 percent, there's-no-arguing-about-it true.

- **Opinions** are what people think of something. Sometimes their opinions are based on facts, and sometimes they aren't.

So if you say, "The United States is a country in North America," that's a fact. But if you say, "The United States is the best country in North America," that's just your opinion. There's no way to prove it. (And someone in Canada or Mexico might disagree with you!)

How do you spot an opinion?

Want to know the telltale words or phrases that show you're hearing someone's opinion instead of a fact? Watch for the following:

> • The phrases *"I believe"* and *"I think."* They're dead giveaways.
>
> • Words like *"always," "never," "most," "least," "usually," "best,"* and *"worst."* These are what we call qualifiers.
>
> • Loaded words, such as calling a dog a *"beast"* instead of an *"animal."* (Which one would you rather pet?)

Someone else's opinion can be helpful—other people can make you look at a conflict in a new and interesting way. Just remember that it is an opinion and not a fact.

Firsthand versus secondhand

There are two basic types of information out there: primary and secondary source. Primary source information comes directly from someone involved in an event. It includes eyewitness accounts, video shot at the scene, data from experiments, personal interviews, and diary entries. Secondary sources are usually based on primary sources. They're interpretations of events, like books or essays about a conflict.

So is a primary source more factual? Not necessarily. A witness can give you the facts about what happened—telling you that a dog bit a kid, for example—but she still has opinions. What if she hates dogs? That negative opinion could change how she states what she saw. She might believe that the dog bit the kid for no reason, even though the kid snatched the dog's bone first.

Whose Lens Are YOU Looking Through?

Every single person has a unique point of view or perspective. (That includes you!) Our perspective is the lens through which we see the world. It's a combination of our experiences, background, and values.

A person's unique perspective is why two people can see the same thing in completely different ways.

Snap judgments

We tend to form an opinion on just about everything the second we come across it. The need to make fast decisions about things is part of who we are as human beings. But when we form an opinion in a hurry, there's a pretty good chance that it has been shaped more by gut feelings and emotions than by facts or clear-headed thinking. That's our bias, and it tends to be shaped by our perspective. People's biases really show when they make arguments for or against things.

All opinions are not created equal

Sometimes bias isn't easy to spot. People don't always come right out and say they love or hate something. But if you can figure out someone's bias you'll have a way easier time deciding whether (or how) to accept what that person is saying. (And this goes a long way toward having an informed opinion.)

So when you come across an opinion, consider who it's coming from.

- **IS IT** a person directly **involved in the conflict**, like a soldier or someone hurt by the fighting?

- **IS IT** a person who feels **a connection** to one of the groups involved in the conflict, like someone who's part of the same ethnic group?

- **IS IT** an expert, like a politics professor or the leader of the UN?

People's connection to a conflict will affect how they see it, what they think of it, and how they talk about it. It doesn't necessarily mean that anyone's take on things is wrong. But people's opinions may be based on emotions more than facts. Sometimes a lot more.

The truth is out there

So if there's just no getting away from bias, why bother reading about a conflict at all? You'll never get the real story, right?

ACTUALLY, THAT'S EXACTLY WHY YOU SHOULD NEVER STOP READING—AND LISTENING AND TALKING WITH OTHERS AND DOING ANYTHING ELSE THAT WILL GIVE YOU ANOTHER VIEW OF AN ISSUE.

Because the truth lies somewhere in the midst of all those stories and different points of view.

And the cool thing is that the more of these "lenses" you use to look at an issue, the more the picture changes and evolves. It never gets old.

Just way more interesting.

Whose Views Are in the NEWS?

Because that's the view you're seeing.

News reporters are people like you and me, and they all have their own unique perspective, too. So do news directors (the people who decide which stories get covered). Their perspectives shape the way they see and share information about events.

Even though newspeople try to be objective—that is, they try not to take sides—it can be pretty hard to keep out bias. It might creep into the language they use to talk about the two sides in a conflict. It can even impact their choice of images to represent a story. This is important, because the way they put together news stories shapes the way we experience them, and that in turn shapes the way we think about conflicts and the people involved in them.

Ter·ror·ism:
The use of violent acts, especially against unarmed people, to create fear in the public.

There's a saying that "One person's terrorist is another's freedom fighter." It's a way of explaining that different people see the same thing in different ways, and that labels change depending on who's placing them. This is why, for example, people in some parts of the world see al-Qaeda members as freedom fighters, standing up to the West, while people in other parts see them as terrorists. So which is it? The answer depends on who you are and how you see the world.

Up close and personal

In some recent wars, like the Iraq War, reporters were allowed to travel with and live among a group of soldiers. That's known as embedding. It sounds like a great way to get at the reality of war, doesn't it? You can't get much closer to the battleground without putting on a uniform yourself.

But a lot of people argue that embedding actually leads to the most biased news reports. It's hard to eat, sleep, talk, laugh, and travel with a group of people 24/7 and not get close to them. A reporter's job, however, is exactly the opposite of that. A reporter is supposed to stay at arm's length from the people in a story to be as objective as possible.

And then there's the fact that news agencies often can't (or don't) embed their reporters with soldiers on both sides. That means that their embedded reporters give audiences only one limited view of a conflict. And that is the very definition of "bias."

PROPAGANDA

Welcome to the art of selling an opinion.

A lot of people—grown-ups included—see violent conflicts as fights between "good guys" and "bad guys." The good guys are right and the bad guys are wrong. It's an easy way of thinking about things that makes it clear who you should root for. A lot of world leaders try to present conflicts this way because they want people to support their side (of course, they're always one of the "good guys"). They use propaganda to try to convince people that this overly simple view of a conflict is the truth.

What is propaganda?

Propaganda plays on people's emotions to influence their opinions, attitudes, or actions. Leaders use it to try to convince people that something is true without actually informing them or making clear, logical arguments to prove it.

In fact, the whole purpose of propaganda is to get people to forget that there are facts or points of view that don't support the message they're selling.

It does that by stirring up strong feelings like fear, anger, excitement, and pride.

Ha! I knew it!

Propaganda works really well when people don't know a lot about the subject, because they're less likely to question what they're seeing and hearing. It's even more effective when it plays on the stereotypes and prejudices they already have, such as "People from that area just love to pick fights." In other words, propaganda reinforces what they already "know," so the message becomes "true."

In the case of conflicts, propaganda often plays on people's ignorance of and serious prejudices about other cultures, nationalities, or religions. Propagandists try to cast the issues as a simple matter of right versus wrong, fair versus unfair, friend versus foe, and especially us versus them. (And it should be pretty obvious by now that things are never that simple!)

Don't believe the hype

Really good propaganda can be tough to spot and even tougher to resist. But trust your gut. If you feel yourself reacting strongly to something, like an expert being interviewed on the news, just stop and think for a moment.

What's the message you're being asked to believe?

Who benefits if you believe it?

Is there another point of view?

✓ The propaganda toolkit

Propagandists use a handful of tricks and tools to create the reaction they want.

Word power

Many words have good or bad feelings attached to them, and those feelings in turn get attached to the propagandist's target.

Monster making

Giving an enemy the face of evil lets people feel like they're the "good guys" fighting the "good fight."

Dazzling opinions

People are more likely to believe messages coming from doctors, scientists, and celebrities.

Plain folks

Messages delivered by everyday people are often seen as trustworthy.

The bandwagon

When people feel that everyone else believes a message, they are more eager to accept it.

Bias

Focusing on only one side of an argument can make it seem stronger. If it's the only side, it must be the right one.

Symbols

Certain objects or images create strong emotions that people transfer to the propagandist's target.

PSSST! Notice anything familiar about these tricks? You should. They're the same ones commercials use (really, what do puppies have to do with toilet paper?). In the end, propaganda is a form of advertising.

The essence of the independent mind lies not in what it thinks, but in how it thinks.

—Christopher Hitchens, author and journalist (1949–2011)

What do YOU think?

By now you've probably figured out that there's more than one way to see the conflicts happening around the world. Even people who spend years studying these conflicts don't always agree on their causes or what could be done to settle them.

But just because the answers aren't always clear or easy to come by, that doesn't mean you should give up looking for them.

The whole point of asking questions—and taking the time to find answers you can trust—is to figure out what you think about what's happening in the world around you. Once you've figured that out, be ready for people to disagree with you, and even to ask you why on earth you think what you do. It's okay if they question your opinion, though, because you'll be ready for them. You'll have facts and solid evidence to support what you think.

Even though you believe in your opinion and can back it up, that doesn't mean you're done. When it comes to building informed opinions, you never are. There's always more information you can think about or new points of view to consider. And when you tell people your opinion, odds are they're going to want to tell you theirs, too.

If a person's opinion happens to be different from yours, that could lead to…wait for it…conflict. But that conflict doesn't have to turn into a shouting match (or worse).

Because the thing about conflicts is, they can turn out to be a good thing if you remember to keep an open mind.

If you're open to new ideas and even the possibility that you might be wrong, you're way more likely to talk it out. And by doing that, you might hear something that leads to an *a-ha!* moment. You could end up seeing the conflict in a new way and understanding it even better than before.

So now what?

Having an informed opinion on a global conflict is great, but you're probably wondering, "What do I do with it?" It's not like you're going to hop the next plane and start negotiating talks in a conflict zone, right?

But what you can do is tell the governments and other groups who are involved in a conflict what you think about it. Let them know you expect them to work hard at finding a solution, whatever you think it might be. You can write letters or emails, sign or start petitions, and just generally spread the word. Help other people become informed global citizens by letting them know about what's happening and why.

Because one thing just about everyone can agree on is, there's no getting away from conflict.

And the more we all understand why and how conflicts come up, the better we can handle them. Together.

SOURCES

"Afghan War." *Encyclopedia Britannica*. Online.

"Afghanistan Profile." *BBC News*, March 5, 2013. Online.

"Afghanistan's Tribal Complexity: Far More than Two Sides to the Conflict." *The Economist*, January 31, 2008. Online.

Bearak, Barry. "Mohammad Zahir Shah, Last Afghan King, Dies at 92." *The New York Times*, July 24, 2007. Online.

Bradshaw, Steve. "*When Good Men Do Nothing.*" *BBC News*, March 30, 2004. Online.

Chalk, Frank. "Radio Propaganda and Genocide." Montreal Institute for Genocide and Human Rights Studies, November 1999. Online.

Cocodia, Jude. "Exhuming Trends in Ethnic Conflict and Cooperation in Africa: Some Selected Cases." *African Journal on Conflict Resolution* 8:3 (2008).

Encyclopedia of the Nations. "The Security Council: Maintaining International Peace and Security." Online.

Gaylord, Chris. "Conflict Minerals: Genocide in Your Gadgets?" *The Christian Science Monitor*, February 24, 2001. Online.

"Genocides, Politicides, and Other Mass Murder Since 1945." Genocide Watch, 2010. Online.

Gilley, Bruce. "Against the Concept of Ethnic Conflict." *Third World Quarterly* 25:6 (2004), 1155–1166. Online.

Goldman, Jason G. "The Psychology of Dictatorship: Kim Jong-Il." *Scientific American*, December 19, 2011. Online.

Goldstein, Joshua S., and Steven Pinker. "War Really Is Going Out of Style." *The New York Times*, December 17, 2011. Online.

Goldstein, Joshua S. "Is War on the Way Out?" *International Relations*. Online.

Goldstein, Joshua S. "Peace on Earth: More than a Wish." *International Relations*. Online.

Goldstein, Joshua S. "Think Again: War; World Peace Could Be Closer than You Think." *Foreign Policy*, Sept/Oct 2011. Online.

"History of Conflict in Afghanistan." *BBC News* video, May 2011. Online.

"How Dictators Keep Control." *Discovery*, December 21, 2011. Online.

Human Security Report Project. "Peace, War, and Numbers: A Nontechnical Guide to Recent Research on the Causes of War and Peace," in Human Security Report 2009/2010: *The Causes of Peace and the Shrinking Costs of War.* New York: Oxford University Press, 2011. Online.

Lovgren, Stefan. "Jerusalem Strife Echoes Ancient History." *National Geographic News*, October 29, 2004. Online.

Marcus, Jonathan. "Jerusalem: Middle East's Oldest Unresolved Conflict." *BBC News*, March 23, 2011. Online.

Marlow, Iain, and Omar El Akkad. "Smartphones: Blood Stains at Our Fingertips." *The Globe and Mail*, December 3, 2010. Online.

NATO. "What is NATO?: An Introduction to the Transatlantic Alliance." Online.

Nobel Foundation, The. "Wars in the 20th Century and Nobel Peace Prize Statistics." Online.

Nusbacher, Aryeh S. *War and Conflict*. Raintree, 2003.

Nye, Joseph S., Jr. "The Benefits of Soft Power." HBS Working Knowledge, August 2, 2004. Online.

Peace Pledge Union. "Talking about Genocides: Rwanda." Online.

"Quick Guide: Afghanistan." *BBC News*, May 20, 2009. Online.

Republic of Rwanda National Unity and Reconciliation Commission. *Training Manual on Conflict Management*. 2006. Online.

Reychler, Luc. "Peace Building Architecture." George Mason University. Online.

"Rwanda: How the Genocide Happened." *BBC News*, December 18, 2008. Online.

"Rwanda Profile: A Chronology of Key Events." *BBC News*, December 27, 2011. Online.

Shah, Anup. "Media, Propaganda, and Rwanda." Global Issues, October 25, 2006. Online.

Smith, Dan. "Trends and Causes of Armed Conflict." Berghof Handbook for Conflict Transformation, August 2004. Online.

Sourt, Caroline. "The Congo's Blood Metals." *The Guardian*, December 25, 2008. Online.

Strauss, Steven D. *The Complete Idiot's Guide to World Conflicts*. 2nd ed. New York: Penguin Group, 2006.

UNESCO. "The Seville Statement." Online.

UNHCR. "Minority Rights Group International." *World Directory of Minorities and Indigenous Peoples—Afghanistan: Pashtuns*, 2008. Online.

United Nations. "Action with Respect to Threats to the Peace, Breaches of the Peace, and Acts of Aggression." Charter of the United Nations. Online.

United Nations. "An Agenda for Peace: Preventive Diplomacy, Peacemaking, and Peacekeeping." June 1992. Online.

United Nations. "Background Note: United Nations Peacekeeping." June 2012. Online.

United Nations Cyberschoolbus. "Peace Education." Online.

United Nations Association in Canada. "The United Nations and the Culture of Peace." Online.

Ury, William. "The Walk from 'No' to 'Yes.'" TED video, October 2010. Online.

Ury, William. "Wandering Out to the Gods: Lessons in Dispute Resolution from the San." *Track Two* 8:1 (July 1999). Online.

Ware, Helen, ed. *The No-Nonsense Guide to Conflict and Peace*. Oxford: New Internationalist Publications, 2006.

Wells, Jennifer. "Coltan a Minefield in the Congo." *The Toronto Star*, July 3, 2011. Online.

Wolff, Stefan. *Ethnic Conflict: A Global Perspective*. New York: Oxford University Press, 2006.

York, Geoffrey. "Plan to Staunch Flow of 'Conflict Minerals' from Congo Causes Turmoil." *The Globe and Mail*, October 21, 2011. Online.

Young, Nigel, ed. *The Oxford International Encyclopedia of Peace*. Oxford: Oxford University Press, 2010.

Zimbardo, Phillip. "The Psychology of Evil." TED video, February 2008. Online.

INDEX

ACKNOWLEDGMENTS

Writing this book changed the way I see the world. I'd like to say a heartfelt thanks to all the big thinkers, activists, and workers on the ground who believe that peace is possible. You've convinced me.

To friends, family, and especially Josh—thank you for your rock-solid support.

Thank you to Mary Beth Leatherdale for the chance to do this book and to Karen Boersma and Jennifer Canham for their careful insights and excellent suggestions. Thanks, in particular, to my editor, John Crossingham, who had the vision and refused to let me off the hook. The many long and challenging conversations, the bits of levity, and your considerable editorial skills made an immeasurable contribution to defining and shaping this book.

A Note from the Author

While developing this book, my editor and I had a lot of discussions about how often we would include information about specific conflicts. In the end, we decided to minimize the examples we used for a couple of key reasons.

First, we wanted this book to offer tools that you could take away to make sense of any conflict, past, present, or future. It's meant to be a guide on how to think about conflicts rather than what to think about particular events or groups around the world.

Second, wars and violent conflicts are highly sensitive subjects, with multiple perspectives on just about every aspect of them. We did not feel we could provide the proper context for considering specific conflicts in a truly fair and balanced way. We respectfully leave it to you to take the message of this book out into the world as you try to make sense of specific wars and conflicts.

Editorial consultants

Erica Chenoweth
Josef Korbel School of International Studies at the University of Denver

Nikki Whaites
International Development Consultant

3 2186 00206 0415

FOSSIL RIDGE PUBLIC LIBRARY DISTRICT
BRAIDWOOD, IL 60408